Filing a Homeowner's Claim:

Natural Disaster or Not

Parker Press Inc.
Briarcliff Manor, NY 10510

ISBN: 978-1-941760-01-7

For the latest information and updates to this material, check out:
http://www.reallifelegal.com/updates

Filing a Homeowner's Claim:

Natural Disaster or Not

Dawn Snyder, Esq.

Real Life Legal™

Helpful Guides for Everyday Legal Matters

Parker Press Inc.

Contents

Contents

What This Book's About

Approximately 65% of Americans own their own homes. Each of these homes is—or should be—covered by a homeowner's insurance policy. Do you know if your policy fully protects you?

Your homeowner's policy might look like a thick stack of boring legalese, but if you ever have damage to your property or injury to a person on it, you'll want to know what it all means. The goal of a homeowner's policy is to cover you against risk. Make sure it does what you want it to.

This book will give you some idea of what a homeowner's insurance policy looks like and what happens when you file your claim. It will introduce you to some experts who can help you in the process, including **"public adjusters,"** attorneys and contractors. It will also give an overview of what happens when there are bumps in the road, like denied claims or insurer bad faith.

Not All Homeowner's Policies Are the Same!

Coverage varies from policy to policy and a claim may be covered under one policy but excluded under another.

Policies can pay claims for everything from a dog bite (with exceptions for certain dog breeds) to a missing roof after a hurricane. Many homeowners are surprised when they find out what their policies do and do not cover. Check with your agent to find out what your policy specifically covers.

If you compare your policy to your neighbor's, they might look alike, but in all likelihood they do not offer exactly the same coverage. That's because insurance policies are boilerplate forms approved by state insurance departments. Some policy provisions are legal in some states and illegal in others.

Insurance companies must have their policies approved in the states in which they are sold. An insurance company can submit each change to its policy forms to the state for approval, or it may instead choose to use certain pre-approved forms. If you are not sure that a policy provision is legal in your state, check with your state insurance department's consumer resources specialists. Some states even make copies of approved forms available online.

Basic Coverages Under a Homeowner's Policy

When it comes to a homeowner's policy, there is no standard "basic coverage." You really have to read the fine print to know what your policy covers. The devil is in the details.

Though it may seem overwhelming, the only way to know what your homeowner's policy covers is to review it. At first it may look like a lot of fine print with no rhyme or reason. But actually policies are organized around what they cover. Typical policy **"coverages"** include:

- **"Dwelling"** usually covers the physical structure of your home and the attached structures like a garage or deck.

- **"Other Structures"** may cover unattached structures other than dwellings, such as sheds and unattached garages.

- **"Personal Property"** or **"Contents"** covers your "things," including clothing and furniture.

- **"Loss of Use"** or **"Additional Living Expenses"** pays for your extra living expenses, like hotel stays, if your home is so damaged that it is uninhabitable or if it will remain so while the home is being repaired.

- **"Medical Payments Coverage"** will pay the medical expenses of someone injured on your property.

- **"Personal Liability Coverage"** pays when someone is injured on your property and you are legally at fault.

Your policy may also include "additional coverages" that can cover you on everything from damage to the trees on your property to protection from credit card fraud. More common homeowner policy add-ons include coverage for water backup, **"endorsements"** for special valuable items (e.g., art, jewelry or furs), and even "green home" coverage to pay for the extra costs involved with making repairs using green technologies and materials.

Protecting Your Home

A homeowner's policy is the best protection for insuring against risk to your property and people on it. It's important to make sure you know what's covered and what's not, before something goes wrong. By then it's too late to get a loss or damage covered.

For most folks, their home is their largest investment. Since insurance protects against risk of loss, it's just good sense to protect your largest investment with a homeowner's policy. If your home is not fully paid off, it's likely that your mortgage lender requires that you keep a current homeowner's policy in place.

Often a homeowner's policy is purchased at the time you first purchase your home, and it's renewed thereafter. If an insurance agent goes over the policy particulars with you, you may be in good shape and know what to expect if a claim arises. All too often, however, when you're buying a home, these matters take backstage as you sign contracts, get ready to close and move.

REAL LIFE EXAMPLE

Barbara was excited to buy a vacation home near the beach in Florida. It's a no-brainer that you need hurricane insurance in Florida, and she was relieved to be outside a flood zone. But the cost of the hurricane insurance was so steep (compared to her regular coverage in Michigan) that she got diverted with that large expense and didn't focus much on the policy details. She just accepted the policy the insurance agent proffered and didn't read it.

A few years after living in the home, Barbara discovered that an undetected slow leak in the refrigerator line had caused the new laminate floors to buckle and grow mold beneath. The damage was so extensive the floor had to be ripped out and replaced at considerable cost. A friend suggested to Barbara that water damage might be covered under her homeowner's policy. When Barbara contacted the insurer, she learned that not only didn't the policy cover water damage, but that for a mere $60 more per year, it could have been covered! Barbara had not been told of this option, nor had she thought to ask. With insurance, the devil is in the details. Lesson learned.

Having a current homeowner's policy in place when disaster strikes can save you from economic ruin. To get paid on a claim, you need to understand the claim process. Both can test your patience and be confusing. Persistence pays.

If you don't keep an up-to-date policy in effect, or if the limits on your policy are too low, the lender can buy a policy to benefit itself and charge you dearly for it. You can read more about these **"lender-placed,"** or **"force-placed"** insurance policies starting on page 26. Regardless of whether you own a policy or the lender mandates and owns it, the terms of the policy determine whether a loss will be covered.

No matter how your policy was obtained, the policy itself is a contract between you and the insurance company. To succeed on a claim under the policy, it helps to know what it covers.

After a catastrophe is a lousy time to discover that "all perils" policies don't cover many natural disasters. For example:

- Most policies cover hail damage but no standard policy will cover floods. A flood policy must be obtained separately through the National Flood Insurance Program, administered by the **"Federal Emergency Management Association (FEMA)."**

- Hurricane damage may be covered if it is from a fire or denied if it is flood related.

- In most states, sinkholes are not covered, but a few states mandate that homeowners' policies cover "catastrophic ground collapse."

If you know ahead of time that your policy does not cover something that you are at special risk for, plan ahead and see if you can obtain an endorsement that provides the coverage.

Special Limitations on Flood Insurance

In many parts of the country, flood insurance is mandatory. It's typically purchased separately and not part of a standard homeowner's policy. Your state may regulate policy availability and coverage terms.

Flood policy coverage is more limited than standard homeowners' policies. For starters, the property and contents coverage must be purchased separately. If a homeowner only buys the dwelling policy, the policy will pay for the damage to the walls, ceiling, and other physical structures, but not personal property damaged in the house.

- Flood policies only pay fair market value, so the homeowner does not get compensated to fully replace the damage.

- The policy is not effective upon signing up; there is a thirty-day waiting period before coverage takes effect.

- The limits are low, only $250,000 for a dwelling and $100,000 for its contents, though homeowners can purchase additional coverage from private insurers.

- Additional coverage is a good idea because repair costs tend to rise when labor and materials are in short supply after a natural disaster. If you have low policy limits, the increased cost of repairs will take a bigger share.

The Homeowner's Policy

If you're having trouble falling asleep, a homeowner's policy may be better than counting sheep. But don't let the legalese take its toll. Make sure you don't find yourself with a packet of fine print that you only really take a hard look at if you need to file a claim.

A complete homeowner's insurance policy often runs thirty pages or more. A policy usually has several parts that cannot be read separately; each must to be read in light of every other section. As a result, policies are very confusing! A loss may appear to be covered based on the wording of one section of the policy but may not ultimately be covered based on language in another section. It's legalese at its worst.

Common Elements of Homeowners' Policies

- **"Declarations Page"**: Name of insured, property address, coverage dates.

- **"Definitions"**: What the big words mean (can be counter-intuitive).

- **"Insuring Agreement"**: What's covered and what's excluded.

- **"Riders"** and **"Endorsements"**: Special add-ons.

Below is a list of these common elements of a homeowner's insurance policy and what kinds of things you can expect to find in each section.

The Declarations Page

This section sets forth the named insured, the address of the insured property, the amount of damage that the policy will cover, the amount of the **"deductible"** and the dates that the policy is in effect. If your date of loss does not fall within the dates listed in the policy terms, it will not be covered, and you will need to look for an older or newer policy that was in effect on that date.

REAL LIFE EXAMPLE

Valerie took possession of her elderly mother Janet's home at the end of April and she immediately called the insurance carrier to arrange to get a policy in place in her own name. Janet's homeowner's policy was effective until May 1st.

The carrier required an inspection before granting a new policy in Valerie's name so it inspected the property in early May. The inspection was successful and the carrier issued a policy effective May 14th. Unfortunately, a storm struck the home on May 5th. Even though the same company insured the home under the old policy and the new policy, the storm was not a covered loss because it occurred during the two weeks between when the old policy lapsed and the new policy went into effect.

Definitions

This section of the policy explains what certain words mean when they are used in the policy. A definitions section is included in many long contracts, but this section can be quite tricky because words don't always mean what you think they mean.

For example, to you the term "family" may include your Aunt Ida who lives three states away, but under the definitions in your policy it will more commonly mean a person who is related to you by blood, marriage or adoption who is also a member of your household.

Definitions can vary from policy to policy. Below are a couple of key policy terms.

- **"Occurrence"**: Many policies require that a loss is only covered if it was caused by an "occurrence." "Occurrence" is typically defined as an accident or an unexpected event. A storm is usually an "occurrence" because it is not expected. Normal aging, on the other hand, is expected and therefore not an "occurrence."

- **"Property damage"**: Your policy probably defines what kind of property damage will be covered. It may also include your loss of the use of the property or loss in value. It could also require direct physical damage, depending on the policy wording.

Keep in mind that even though a word appears in the "Definitions" section of your policy, the item may still not be covered under that policy. For example, your policy may define a word like "pollutants," which is then used in the "exclusions" section to say that the policy does not cover damage caused by them. If you only read the "Definitions," you may mistakenly believe that damage caused by pollutants is covered.

Insuring Agreement

This is the vital section of your policy which informs you in what situations the insurance carrier will pay a claim under the policy. It contains the **"Coverages"** and the **"Exclusions."**

- **Coverages** lists what losses (if caused by an "occurrence") are covered. Some homeowners run into a problem by believing that a loss will be covered by the policy because it was not excluded. But if the loss is not listed in the "Coverages," then it does not matter that the loss is not excluded; a loss must be covered before it can be excluded.

- **Exclusions** list the types of loss that are specifically not covered under the policy. Even if a type of losses is listed under "Coverages," an exclusion can knock it out and you won't get paid for the claim.

The fact that an occurrence is not "excluded" does not mean it's covered. Also, a loss doesn't have to be excluded to not be covered.

Making Sense of Exclusions

Some common exclusions include mold damage, flooding, age-related deterioration, intentional damage caused by a resident, sewage backup, power outages and war or terrorism. If these types of losses are excluded under your policy, you may be able to purchase a **"rider"** or separate coverage for an excluded risk.

Flood insurance must be purchased separately through the National Flood Insurance Program, which is managed by FEMA and found at http://www.floodsmart.gov.

Under most policies, a covered loss must be caused by an occurrence, or an unexpected accident. "Wear and tear," which is a common exclusion, is a good example of something not caused by an "occurrence" and not covered. So even if wear and tear are not specifically excluded, a typical policy will not cover age-related damage because it is expected. It is not caused by an occurrence.

Not all policies list the same exclusions, or even list the common exclusions in the same way. Consider, for example, water damage:

- Some policies will not cover water damage at all, no matter how it occurs.

- Some policies will cover water damage if it is the result of a covered occurrence like a burst pipe or a broken appliance.

- Other policies will specifically spell out situations in which water damage is covered, like when a hole is torn in the roof as a result of an occurrence and water enters the building through it.

Riders and Endorsements

"Riders" and "endorsements" are basically the same thing: a document providing additional terms or coverages. These clauses cover "special additional terms," that can remove or add coverage. For example, a rider might provide that there is no coverage for a loss if the home is unoccupied for a stated number of days. A rider might limit the amount of money that you can recover for a loss to a certain percentage.

Riders and endorsements sometimes look like separate documents but they are still a part of the policy and may modify other terms. If sewage backup is excluded under a homeowner policy, a homeowner may be able to purchase an endorsement covering it. Other common endorsements or riders that homeowners purchase include:

- Additional coverage for especially valuable jewelry, items or equipment.

- Home business coverage.

- Coverage for damage from mine and land subsidence (underground collapse of a mine).

Policies Don't Cover Wear and Tear

Many homeowners think a homeowner's policy will pay out when anything goes wrong with their home. But in fact a homeowner's policy protects against something sudden and accidental, not routine wear and tear. Just as an auto policy will not reimburse you to replace worn brake pads, a homeowner's policy will not pay for replacement of a thirty-year-old roof that leaks.

Force-placed (Lender-placed) Insurance

Your mortgage lender may require you to keep adequate insurance on your home, because they want to protect their interest. If you don't buy the insurance, they may do so and you could be in for a few surprises: what it costs and what is (and isn't) covered!

Mortgage lenders require that homeowners keep adequate insurance on their mortgaged property. This requirement is to protect the lender's investment if the home is damaged or destroyed. If you don't have a policy in place or it is insufficient, the lender can buy one known as a **"force-placed"** policy. A lender-placed policy might sound like a good idea on the surface but there are big drawbacks.

Downside to Lender-placed Policies

- The policy price is added to the amount of your loan.

- If you do not pay the added cost, the lender can foreclose on your home to recover it.

- These policies cost two to ten times more than a traditional policy and tend to offer minimal coverage.

- Coverage tends to be limited to major catastrophic events such as fires.

- Common coverages, for personal property inside the home and/or liability for injury to someone on your property, are not covered.

- Carriers on these policies work for the lender, not the homeowner, and this can make claims issues a nightmare.

Some lender-placed policies are dual interest, which means they protect both the lender and the homeowner and may pay **"replacement cost"** for the dwelling. But others only protect the lender. In that case, claim payments are limited to the balance remaining on the mortgage loan. This leaves the homeowner at a loss for any equity in the home and any damaged contents.

Avoid Force-placed Policies

Government and consumer groups have taken notice of lender-placed policies. In January 2014, the **"Consumer Financial Protection Bureau (CFPB)"** added regulations that require mortgage companies to inform homeowners before charging them for this insurance. In late 2013, the State of New York proposed major reforms to prevent carriers from paying premium-inflating kickbacks to mortgage companies for the sale of force-placed insurance policies. Lender-placed insurance practices are under scrutiny and homeowners should do what they can to avoid these policies.

How to Stay Clear of Lender-placed Insurance

Lender-placed insurance is avoidable by abiding by the terms of your mortgage contract:

- Maintain continuous coverage.

- Make sure the coverage meets the minimum amount required by your loan documents.

- Review your policy to confirm that the lender is listed on it and that the lender's information is correct.

Sometimes lenders incorrectly charge a homeowner for force-placed insurance when the homeowner already has a valid policy in effect. If this happens to you, give the lender evidence of coverage. The lender must then have the force-placed policy canceled. If your coverage was adequate and continuous, the lender will refund the payments it charged you for the time that your coverage was in compliance.

If you run into trouble having the lender-placed policy removed even after complying with the loan requirements, contact your state's department of insurance for help.

A Walk Through the Claims Process

When your home floods because of a burst pipe, or you're hard hit by a big storm, you're likely starting the claims process. Whether you know it or not, it's important to start documenting your loss from that moment on.

A loss begins when an "occurrence" happens and causes damage. In some cases, the damage is sudden and obvious. In others, it is gradual and virtually unnoticeable. In either case, the first step of the claims process is to notify the insurance company. And this isn't just being smart; it's also a contractual requirement under your policy.

If your property is damaged and you need to file an insurance claim, follow the requirements listed in your policy. If you don't, the claim might not be paid.

Insurance policies spell out a policyholder's duties after loss. If you don't comply with these duties, you will be in breach of your insurance policy. This can jeopardize coverage for the claim.

Document the Damage

It's essential to document the damage as much as you can to support your claim. In this context, a picture is worth more than a thousand words. For example:

- Take photographs before moving anything at the scene.

- Include some photos shot from a distance away so that the adjuster will be able to see the overall view and confirm that the photos are of your home and not someone else's.

- Try to include your address in some exterior shots as well.

Protect Against Further Damage

You also need to preserve the property to prevent further damage. Use common sense! For example:

- If a storm tears off a part of the roof, put a tarp over the exposed areas to prevent water from doing further damage.

- If the pillar holding up a corner of your porch is knocked loose, add reinforcement as soon as possible to keep it from collapsing.

Insurance adjusters are on the lookout for fraud. It helps make their job easier if you can give them solid evidence of the damage. It will make processing and paying your claim go more smoothly.

Keep Track of Your Expenses

If you pay for supplies or labor for the emergency repairs, save the receipts and provide those to your insurance company. Proof documenting repairs can also become crucial later if the same property is damaged again.

REAL LIFE EXAMPLE

Shelly filed an insurance claim for hail damage to her siding and the roof of her porch. The insurance company denied the claim, stating that she had made a claim for the same damage three years earlier. Shelly was able to provide the adjuster with receipts for the repairs for the earlier damage, along with the contractor's certificate of completion certifying that the repairs listed in the prior claim were completed. With the proof that the earlier storm damage had been repaired, the insurance company approved Shelly's hail storm claim.

Checklist for Filing an Insurance Claim

1. Read your policy to see what is required to report and file a claim.

2. Preserve the property to prevent further damage.

3. Document the damage to prove your claim, primarily through the use of photographs that show the damage and confirm the location is your property.

4. Retain receipts for supplies and labor needed for emergency repairs.

5. File a claim with proper supporting documentation.

Reporting a Claim

Whether you wake up in the middle of the night to the sound of a car hitting your garage or you notice damage that seems to be getting worse after a storm, you must give "prompt" notice of the loss to the carrier or risk violating the terms of your policy.

In some states, an insurance company cannot deny coverage based on late notice unless it can show that it was harmed by the lateness. In other states, a homeowner's late notice creates a presumption that the carrier was prejudiced; the homeowner can attempt to rebut the presumption by presenting expert evidence to show that the carrier was not prejudiced.

If you believe you may have a claim, your best course of action is to provide notice to your insurance company as soon you believe there may be a covered loss.

You have two options for giving notice. You can notify the carrier directly or you can notify the agent who sold you the policy. To notify the carrier, you can call their claims hotline, submit an online claim report, or follow some other means allowed by the carrier. In many states, notice to the insurance agent is legally the same as notice to the insurance company.

When you file the claim, the process will be quicker and easier if you have your policy number handy. You should receive a claim number right away and you will need to include it on anything you send to the insurance company. Some insurance companies will tell you who your adjuster is and schedule an inspection immediately. Other companies will have the adjuster call you later to set up an inspection date and time.

Insurance policies include language that requires the policy holder (a.k.a. "first-party claimant") to cooperate. If you don't, you can be found in breach of the policy and the insurance company might not pay the claim.

You Have a Duty to Cooperate

When insurance companies investigate claims, they sometimes request:

- Follow-up inspections by experts.
- Additional documents for you to provide.
- Recorded statements concerning the claim.
- Examinations under oath (EUO).

Inspection by an Insurance Adjuster

Once the claim is filed, the insurance company will set up a date and time to inspect the damage. If the date and time are not set when you filed your claim, an adjuster will call you to schedule one.

The adjuster will review the damage and take photos and measurements to prepare an estimate. The adjuster can be an employee of the insurance company or an employee of a separate company which provides this expertise.

- An adjuster working directly for the insurance carrier is a **"staff adjuster."**

- An adjuster who works for an outside company (not your carrier) is referred to as an **"independent adjuster."**

If the field adjuster who shows up for your inspection is a staff adjuster, that person will usually be your company contact throughout the claims process. If the inspection is done by an independent adjuster, then the insurance company will assign an in-house rep to answer your questions and address any problems.

It is a good idea to be home for the inspection. If there is interior damage then you need to either be home or have someone there to let the adjuster in. If the damage is only to the outside of the home, make sure the adjuster has access to the damaged area. For example, it's a good idea to unlock any gates and keep dogs on leashes.

Be Sure You Are Home for a Damage Inspection

Even if you are not required to be home for the inspection, it's a good idea to be there. Here's why:

- You can answer questions and point out less obvious damage.

- You can get a sense of other documentation that may be required to prove your claim.

If you have a contractor or a public adjuster on board, consider having them present for the inspection as well.

Calculating Your Insurance Recovery

Part of the claims process is finalizing the extent of repairs and finalizing an estimate on the cost to fix them. Negotiating may be important here.

After the inspection, the adjuster will provide you with an estimate to restore the damaged property or **"scope,"** which is short for "scope of repairs." The length of time it takes to receive the scope varies from company to company. Sometimes an adjuster will prepare the estimate on site, perhaps heading back to his or her van to enter notes into a computer, and returning in a short while with a copy of an estimate for you. In other cases, the adjuster will prepare the estimate at the office and mail a copy to you days or weeks later.

Laws Regulate Insurer Response Time

Each state has rules that regulate how insurance companies can respond to claims. These rules may set timetables for the carrier to provide the scope, the settlement check, and any other documentation that the carrier needs from the policyholder in order to complete the claim.

Your state may have set a deadline requiring that the carrier provide the estimate to you within a certain number of days. Depending on whether the carrier will also require **"proof of loss,"** discussed next, the estimate may also arrive along with the check for the amount of the claim payment.

Proof of Loss

Sometimes insurance policies require that you file a **"proof of loss"** before a claim will be paid. This is a sworn statement the homeowner must file within a certain amount of time as stated in the policy, commonly either sixty days from the date of loss or from the date of the company's request for proof of loss. If claimants fail to file proof of loss on time, they may be unable to sue the insurance company for any issue related to the claim.

A proof of loss is a sworn statement attesting to the damages. It includes details about the event that caused the loss, ownership details about the property involved, and specific dollar amounts for each element of the damage claimed.

A proof of loss is a big deal! Most states make it a crime to "knowingly falsify material facts" in order to fraudulently recover under the insurance policy. Usually it is a felony. Some states also make it a tort, which means that the insurance carrier can sue you for damages as well. The policy will clearly provide words to the effect: "We will not provide coverage for all or any part of a loss if, before or after the loss, any insured has committed fraud."

The courts in some jurisdictions take a homeowner-friendly position on this type of fraud law and allow a homeowner to recover portions of a claim that were presented truthfully. Others allow a carrier to void the policy entirely if the insured commits any fraud.

Anatomy of a Scope

The insurer's scope is a summary of the carrier's investigation and the information it is based upon. It will also estimate how much money the insurer calculates it will take to repair the property, with pricing details.

A scope typically lists the key information related to the claim. These items are discussed in more detail in the sections that follow.

Claim Number	Policy Number
Insured	Date of Loss
Property Address	Date of Inspection
Deductible	Replacement Cost for Claim
Depreciation (Recoverable/Not)	Total Amount of Claim

How a Claim Payment Is Calculated

Most policies provide payment based on **"actual cash value (ACV)"** or replacement cost. Replacement cost is the amount it would cost to: (1) replace the item today with a similar quality item or (2) repair the property with a comparable material. ACV is the fair market value, or resale value, of the item and is calculated by taking the replacement cost and deducting **"depreciation."** Less common policies offer other claim valuation variations including payment based on "equivalent construction."

If the damage is extensive, the scope will give a room-by-room breakdown of measurements, materials and labor costs to repair the damage. It will factor in the quality and condition of the property before the loss. So if a home has storm damage to the roof, the scope will itemize the measurements and quality of the damaged shingles and estimate the material and labor costs to restore the damage to its pre-loss condition.

Calculating a Loss

The terms of your policy will determine how the carrier will calculate the loss payment. The most common ways and optional upgrades include:

- **Replacement Cost:** Compensation for the full cost to replace or repair the damaged property.

- **ACV** or **Actual Cash Value:** This is also known as fair market value, or the amount that a willing buyer would have paid for the property just before the loss. Not all carriers calculate ACV the same way, but it is basically the replacement cost minus depreciation.

- **Extended Replacement Cost:** This lets you replace the covered property even if the cost exceeds the policy coverage limit up to a certain percentage. If a rise in construction costs makes the repair cost more than the policy limit, this coverage provides that the carrier will still pay for it, often up to 120 or 125% of the stated coverage limit.

- **A1** and **A2** coverage is a less common model of tiered coverage.

  - A1 policies provide for "similar," like-kind and -quality repairs as in a more common replacement cost policy.

  - A2 coverage provides only "common" construction "of the damaged part." For example, consider a home with a slate roof that is damaged in a storm. Under an A1 policy, the homeowner may receive a new slate roof of like kind and quality to what was on the house before the storm. Under an A2 policy, only the damaged shingles would be replaced, and not necessarily with slate because that is not common nor used in standard new construction.

- **Building Code Upgrade:** With this coverage, the insurer will pay the extra cost to repair or rebuild the damage according to the current building code. Homeowners don't need to rebuild their house every time the building code changes, but when a part of the building does need to be repaired or rebuilt, the rebuilding must comply with the current code. Without building code upgrade coverage, homeowners are left footing the bill for the extra repairs.

REAL LIFE EXAMPLE

Evan's roof was damaged in a wind storm. The insurance carrier agreed that the damage was caused by the storm and covered under the policy. But the damage was to the third layer of shingles and local code only allowed three layers of roof. The roof was too brittle to be repaired without tearing off the old roof. Because Evan's policy did not have building code upgrade coverage, he had to pay the cost of tearing off the old roof, out of pocket.

Calculating Actual Cash Value Claims

Total damages related to covered loss
- Deductible
- Non-recoverable depreciation
- Recoverable depreciation
= Claim amount

For example, if a storm damages a roof that had some age-related wear and tear before the storm, the claim might look like this:

Roof damage: $8,000
Minus deductible: $500
Minus non-recoverable depreciation: $200
Minus recoverable depreciation: $1,850
= Claim amount: $5,450

What is Depreciation?

"Depreciation" is value lost over time through normal aging, wear and tear, maintenance or neglect, and obsolescence. Insurance companies follow formulas to calculate depreciation. If an item has a life expectancy of ten years, it loses 10% of its value each year. If the item is destroyed when it is three years old, then the depreciation would be 30%.

You may or may not be paid for the depreciation of your property. It depends on the terms of your policy. A policy with replacement cost coverage will pay the amount to replace or repair the property. For example, assume your kitchen appliances, which are five years old, are all damaged in a flood, a replacement policy would cover the cost to buy new appliances at today's prices. By contrast, an actual cash value or ACV policy would pay you the value of your kitchen appliances, with five years of depreciation. In short, An ACV insurance policy will pay the cost to repair or replace property based on the replacement cost minus the depreciation.

Recoverable Depreciation

With a replacement cost homeowner's insurance policy, you can recover some or all of the depreciation withheld by the carrier. The carrier will provide upfront payment for the ACV and retain the payment for depreciation. It will issue a second payment for the depreciation when the property is actually repaired or replaced.

- **Damaged Contents.** Depreciation is withheld on damaged contents. It is paid when the item is replaced so the carrier will issue a first payment for the ACV soon after the loss. To issue the depreciation check, it will need receipts to show that the item has actually been replaced.

- **Damage to Dwelling.** Each carrier has different rules to recover depreciation for repairs to property. Under some policies, a homeowner must give proof that the repairs are either two-thirds or 80% complete. Under others, the carrier may release the depreciation before the repairs are complete, if it receives a copy of a contract that the homeowner has signed with a qualified contractor to complete the repairs detailed in the scope. This is good for the homeowner, who then does not need to front the payment for the repairs while waiting to receive the depreciation payment.

How to Recover Depreciation

The carrier's scope should tell you how to recover the depreciation that it withholds. This generally means you have to:

1. Have all of the repairs made according to the scope.

2. Provide proof to the carrier. This can include photographs of the property, receipts, and a contractor's certificate of completion.

3. Pay attention to deadlines. With some insurers, the repairs must be made as soon as 180 days from date of loss, while others require that they be made within two years.

Repairing the Damage

If you're finalizing an insurance claim, odds are that you'll hire a contractor to help with the work. Consider your options carefully, as they may impact whether your insurance covers the damage.

The purpose of the claim payment is to allow you to have the damage fixed. A smart first move is to have two or three contractors bid on the work in the scope. The insurance company might have a list of preferred contractors. Some states have a rule stating that the carrier is not allowed to tell you which contractor to use, so the preferred contractor list is just a suggestion and can be a good place to start to get one of your bids.

Using the Insurance Company's Preferred Contractor

A **"preferred contractor"** is one that the insurance company recommends. To the contractor, the insurance company is a good source of steady business. This can be good for a homeowner because a preferred contractor has a lot of business on the line, so there is incentive for these contractors to get the job done well and on budget. They know angry homeowners will complain to the carrier and that this will hurt their business.

You may be wary that a preferred contractor will avoid rocking the boat with the insurance company by disagreeing with the scope or estimated cost. This is one reason it makes sense to solicit bids from one or two independent contractors as well.

Pros and Cons of Using an Insurer's "Preferred Contractor"

- **Pros:** They get a lot of business from the carrier and have reason to keep customers happy.

- **Cons:** They may hesitate to disagree with a scope, and instead cut corners to earn more profit.

- **Recommendation:** Get one or two independent bids to learn value and adequacy of scope.

Choose a contractor who has experience in your geographic area. Each municipality has its own building codes. Even the climate and geography present different construction challenges. A non-local contractor may not know which building materials and techniques are needed to stand the test of time in your area.

The damage repair stage is quicker and easier if the contractor has an understanding of the claims process and a good working relationship with the insurance company. If, for example, you do need a supplement on your claim, a good contractor can explain the reasons to the adjuster and smooth the process so you can get the extra payment approved quickly.

REAL LIFE EXAMPLE

Andrew's roof was damaged in a wind storm and he hired an out-of-state contractor to fix it. The contractor moved temporarily into Andrew's neighborhood after the major storm. But the contractor was not familiar with the specifics of the building code in Andrew's city and obtained the wrong permit. Because Andrew was the homeowner, the building department issued building code violations to Andrew. Even though the repairs were complete before he received the notice, Andrew needed to jump through hoops to obtain the correct permit in order to avoid civil prosecution by the city.

Whose Name Is on the Settlement Check?

If you have a mortgage on your home, the name of the bank or mortgage company will be included on the settlement check.

- Before you can cash the check or pay a contractor, the bank will need to endorse the check and then it may send the endorsed check back to you or it may, instead, deposit the check into an escrow account and issue payments as the costs are incurred.

- If you have retained a lawyer or other consultant, your contract with them may require that they be added on the settlement check as well.

Don't Forget Your Deductible

Even "covered losses" are not paid 100% by an insurance policy. If you have a $500 deductible, then you have to pay out of pocket for $500 worth of repair or replacement costs. You may be able to do some of the minor repair work yourself to "recoup" the deductible.

For example, if a leak requires a bedroom to be repainted and you choose to do it yourself, you may save $500 you would otherwise have had to pay a painter! You can save the cost of paying for a contractor for the amount of the deductible and still get the repairs completed as listed in the scope. Remember to save all receipts for the materials and take some photos to forward to the insurance adjuster to show that the damage was fixed.

Supplementing the Claim Payment

Material and labor prices change. New damage can be discovered once repairs start. For one reason or another, sometimes the insurance carrier's estimate just is not enough money to finish the repairs in the scope. When this happens, you can request a supplement from the carrier.

If the Settlement Doesn't Cover the Repairs

If the check is insufficient, ask the insurer for a "supplement" before having the work done. Insurance companies usually state clearly that they will deny requests for a supplement if it's not made before the repairs are done.

My Claim is Denied—Now What?

In a perfect world, your legitimate claim will be approved quickly. In the real world, the insurer will scrutinize your coverage and your claim and may find a reason to deny coverage.

It should come as no surprise that not all insurance claims are approved. When a claim is denied, the carrier should tell the policyholder the reason in a "denial letter." Your state's department of insurance has rules that mandate what must be covered in a denial letter. Typically the carrier must state the basis for the denial and the relevant policy language that applies.

An insurance adjuster has the duty to look for coverage if it exists. But sometimes the coverage is denied. This can happen if:

- There just is no damage caused by the occurrence.

- The damage is excluded under the policy.

- The insurer is acting in bad faith in denying the claim.

If you suspect the carrier is wrongfully denying coverage, consider hiring a lawyer who specializes in policyholder rights.

No Damage?

When a major storm hits an area, homeowners sometimes assume that there is damage to their property. If siding is blown off the side of the house then damage can be easy to see. But it can take a trained eye to find less obvious damage. Each home, policy and claim is different so don't assume your home has damage because a neighbor's does.

Victor filed an insurance claim for hail damage from a 2013 storm. The adjuster noted that there was hail damage to the soft metals around his roof but no evidence of hail to the window casings. The window casings had been replaced after a 2009 hail damage claim. The adjuster checked the records of a storm reporting service; its report showed that in Victor's neighborhood, hail in the 2013 storm was not large enough to cause the damage to the roof metals. An independent roofer that the insurance company called in to review the findings agreed and the claim was denied.

If you believe the damage you see is related to a covered loss and the adjuster does not see it, consider having someone with construction experience look at it. When a contractor or engineer can document and explain the damage to the insurance company, homeowners sometimes reverse the carrier's decision, finding the coverage.

Why Is Damage Excluded?

Claims are denied when the loss falls under the policy's coverage exclusions. If the damage was caused entirely by an excluded peril then there is no question—the damage is not covered under the policy. The question gets trickier when there is more than one cause.

One of the most common exclusions is wear and tear. If your thirty-year shingles are on year twenty-eight, they are nearing the end of their useful life and probably showing signs of age. If they are already brittle and crumbling, a violent storm may be the final blow that causes the roof to fall in. The wording of the policy determines whether the damage is covered.

Policies take different approaches to concurrent causes. Some exclude any damage that was caused in any way, directly or indirectly, by an excluded loss. Under one of those policies, the crumbling shingles would not be covered.

Other policies exclude the damage only if the proximate, or most direct, cause of the damage was excluded. This is known as the **"efficient proximate cause"** rule. A few states have adopted the efficient proximate cause rule and it applies there regardless of what the policy states. In this case, the roof damage would be covered if the storm was the most direct cause of the loss.

What Happens When Things Go South?

If your claim is denied, it's not the end. Policies typically afford a review process to resolve claim disputes. Read the fine print to see what this involves under your policy. Sometimes arbitration or mediation is required.

Insurance policies list the dispute resolution options available to the policyholder in case of a disagreement. Though each dispute resolution forum has its own set of rules and trade-offs, alternative dispute resolution forums are usually quicker and more cost-efficient than traditional lawsuits. The most common are appraisal and mediation or arbitration.

Insurance adjusters sometimes don't see the same thing that the homeowner sees. Again, policy language is the key.

Settling a Denied Claim:
The Appraisal Clause

Hidden deep in the "Conditions" section of many homeowners' insurance policies is an "appraisal" clause. Appraisal is a dispute resolution method that is favored in the insurance industry. It can be an effective form of dispute resolution, but not all homeowners know about it.

A typical appraisal clause says that if the insured and the carrier fail to agree on the amount of loss, either party may demand an appraisal. Each side then selects an independent appraiser and the two appraisers select an impartial umpire. If the appraisers fail to agree on the amount of loss then they submit their differences to the umpire to decide. When a policyholder and insurer disagree, appraisal is a quicker and less expensive way for each side to resolve it than filing a lawsuit.

In some states, carriers participate in appraisal to determine whether there is coverage. In other states, carriers will only submit on the issue of damage amount—once they determine a claim is indeed covered. If a carrier won't submit to appraisal on the issue of coverage, the next step is litigation to settle the dispute. You have to check to see how appraisal is used in your policy and your state.

Mediation and Arbitration

You may hear these two terms lumped together but mediation and arbitration are separate animals. Either can be included in your policy's "Conditions" as a form of dispute resolution, but both are less common than appraisal clauses. These clauses may change your right to sue the carrier.

Mediation

In **"mediation,"** a neutral third party helps the parties reach an agreement. The process tends to be less formal. The parties are usually separated while the mediator travels back and forth to speak with each party privately until they can reach an agreement. Mediation can be an effective first step to avoid litigation. It is voluntary, and the parties can still go to court if they do not settle at mediation.

State Mediation for Major Disaster Claims

The states themselves get involved in mediation when there are natural disasters and massive damage. For example, in 2013, New York and New Jersey selected the American Arbitration Association (AAA) to oversee volunteer mediation programs to resolve Hurricane Sandy storm claims. These programs allowed homeowners to request mediation to settle disputes with insurance carriers for Sandy-related homeowner's, auto, or commercial insurance claims.

The American Arbitration Association was also selected by the states of Louisiana and Mississippi to administer mediation programs to settle disputes over claims arising from Hurricanes Katrina and Rita. According to the AAA, it mediated over 17,000 cases in those programs, with nearly three-quarters of those cases reaching a settlement. This means more than 10,000 policyholders were able to avoid the time and expense of a lawsuit to settle their claims.

Arbitration

Compared to mediation, arbitration is much more court-like. With **"arbitration,"** each side presents its case and an arbitrator or panel of arbitrators issues a binding decision. An important difference from mediation is that arbitration replaces litigation. When there is a valid and enforceable arbitration clause in an insurance policy, the policyholder waives the right to sue. Arbitration awards are binding and not often overturned by a court.

An insurance company cannot force an insured homeowner to arbitrate unless the policy contains an arbitration clause. But if there is an arbitration clause, the homeowner typically cannot sue the carrier in court for a dispute over a claim; the dispute must be settled by arbitration.

Some benefits of arbitration are saving time and expense and the need for experts. The proceedings tend to be quicker and overall less expensive than court actions. Arbitrators often understand the issues better than a jury, which can quickly become bored by hours of dull policy language.

Arbitration fees are structured differently than traditional lawsuit expenses. With arbitration, the bulk of expenses are incurred upfront. In a regular lawsuit, fees grow larger as the matter progresses. An arbitration demand filing fee can be in the thousands of dollars and there are relatively few fees after that. However, the cost can vary from case to case. Plus, policy language, state rules or special consumer-focused arbitration rules sometimes shift the cost to the insurer so that a homeowner's costs for the proceeding are minimal.

Insurance Bad Faith

For the idealists among us, it may seem far-fetched that an insurance company would deny a legitimate claim. But it happens and you have options if it happens to you.

Insurance companies are regulated by states and they usually behave themselves. When they don't, it is called **"insurance bad faith."** In most states, when an insurance company acts in bad faith, it may face punitive damages. If you suspect your insurance carrier is acting in bad faith, you would be wise to speak with a lawyer to discuss your options.

States Regulate Insurance Claims

Most states have laws that mandate how insurance carriers handle claims. In some states these are broad laws that apply to many types of businesses. In others, they are specific to insurance companies.

- State laws may be called "Unfair Claims Settlement Practices Act" or "Unfair Insurance Practices Act."

- State insurance laws may regulate: deadlines the carriers must follow, how they must value claims, and what information they must provide to a homeowner.

What Is "Insurance Bad Faith?"

Insurance companies owe their policyholders a duty of good faith and fair dealing. When an insurance company breaches this duty, you may have a claim against them in court. This claim is in addition to a claim that you may have against the insurer for breaching the contract to provide insurance.

To protect policyholders, state lawmakers define certain actions as "bad faith." The following are considered acts of bad faith:

- Failure to acknowledge it has received a claim.

- Failure to investigate a claim fully and within a reasonable amount of time.

- Lies about relevant facts or what the policy covers.

- Failure to communicate regularly or acknowledge it has received important communications.

- Denial of a claim based on a specific policy provision without explaining the reason.

- Misrepresentation of policy coverage by offering a settlement that does not include all of the eligible amounts.

- Threats to prolong the arbitration process to coerce a policyholder into accepting a lower settlement offer.

- Failure to inform the claimant within a required time that it has accepted or rejected the claim.

What to Do About Carrier Bad Faith

If the insurance company is not handling your claim fairly, you do have options. Some of the most effective actions are:

1. Request a different adjuster.

2. Seek help from the state department of insurance.

3. Consider filing a lawsuit.

Often policy holders only have a limited period of time, like one year from the date of loss, to file a claim-related suit against the carrier. That deadline, which is like a "statute of limitations," is not extended while you wait for a resolution without filing suit.

Ask for a Different Adjuster

Insurance companies act through their employees. When customers are treated unfairly, it is usually not because of a company policy, but rather a problem employee. Changing the employee can often fix the problem.

A field adjuster is a homeowner's main insurance company contact for a claim. Occasionally an overzealous adjuster will work against a homeowner, looking for reasons to deny the claim. When this happens, going above the adjuster to his or her supervisor to request a new adjuster will sometimes solve the problem.

REAL LIFE EXAMPLE

Charles filed an insurance claim for storm damage to his siding and roof. The field adjuster was rude and threatened that the company would cancel his policy if Charles did not drop the claim. Then the adjuster denied the claim, stating that there was no damage visible. Charles had his contractor take photos of the damage, and he sent them to the adjuster's supervisor, along with a complaint about how the adjuster had treated him. The supervisor was appalled by her employee's unprofessional behavior and scheduled a reinspection with another adjuster, who subsequently did find damage.

Speak with Your State Department of Insurance

State insurance departments aim to protect their residents. One way they do this is by setting up hotlines and websites for consumers to report unfair actions by insurance companies.

- A state department of insurance will step in to make sure that carriers are following its consumer protection rules.

- An insurance company has great incentive to cooperate with an insurance department because it does not want to lose its license to do business in that state.

For some consumers, contacting the department of insurance can help them get the response they need from the carrier. The California Department of Insurance, for instance, announced that in 2013 it recovered more than $62.7 million for consumers through its investigations of consumer complaints and examinations of insurance company market conduct.

Consider Filing a Lawsuit

If your insurance carrier is not following the rules for fair settlement practices, consider speaking to a lawyer. A lawyer with insurance experience can evaluate your situation and tell whether it would be worthwhile and possible to file suit against the carrier.

A lawyer should review your policy to determine whether: (1) your case is strong enough to warrant a lawsuit and (2) whether you are bound to go to arbitration first.

Many lawyers offer a free consultation before you sign on as a client. If they are filing a lawsuit on your behalf, it is common for lawyers to represent you on a contingency arrangement.

When it comes to lawsuits, the process is a punishment no matter who wins the case. A civil case can easily last two years or more, cost you lost wages for depositions and court appearances, and violate your privacy when the carrier's lawyers dig into your finances, prior unrelated criminal convictions, and even what you ate for lunch on the day of the loss.

Of course, even if you win the case, you will not be reimbursed for the time you invested in it, the hidden expert, mediation, and other fees, or the stress and anxiety that litigation triggers.

How a Contingency Fee Works

With a **"contingency fee,"** a percentage of the settlement is paid to your lawyers as their fee.

- You do not pay upfront for the lawyer's time.

- Win or lose, you may be on the hook for legal expenses.

- Clarify how the fee will work, if you are not sure.

Expenses can add up! They include things like witness fees, deposition costs, transcripts and large photocopying bills.

Should I Hire a Professional to Submit My Claim to an Insurer?

There is no "one size fits all" when it comes to hiring a professional to help. Often it depends on what you want to handle on your own and the type of claim you have.

Every day, homeowners successfully file and negotiate insurance claims on their own. But sometimes it helps to have a professional involved. Different types of professionals offer different benefits but they come at a price. Make sure you evaluate the cost and the benefit of hiring someone to help.

Sometimes having a professional on board to help with the process will only add another layer to the communication, and the fees involved may hurt your bottom line.

When to Hire a Professional to Submit a Claim

A professional can help maximize your recovery in certain situations:

- Large, complicated claims.
- Claims with coverage questions.
- Adjuster is unreasonable or acting in bad faith.
- You are required to give a statement under oath.

In some situations a professional may be the best person to handle a claim. For example, with a natural disaster, there can be a lot of damage and many people filing claims. Or you could have a unique or special property with values that do not fit into a standard valuation computer program. You want to be sure your interests are protected and not undervalued by the insurance company. That's when a professional can help.

Similarly if there is a question whether there is coverage for the loss, having someone with expertise to act as an advocate can help you present your strongest claim. A difficult adjuster who is unreasonable or acting in bad faith may also raise the alarm bell that it's time to hire a professional.

Sometimes with an out-of-state carrier, you want a buffer between you and the insurance company. A professional with knowledge of the state's insurance rules and the homeowner's policy terms can be invaluable in getting a more effective settlement, but be sure to understand the "professional's" fee!

If the carrier requests an "examination under oath (EUO)," that means they're looking for a statement that will hold up in court. In fact, these sworn statements have the same weight as testimony in court. If a carrier requests an EUO, get yourself a lawyer.

Disadvantages of Hiring a Professional

Experts come with a price tag. The fees will vary based on the type of professional and the situation of the claim. Some, such as lawyers and public adjusters, may work on a contingency arrangement. Others, such as engineering experts, may need to be paid regardless of the outcome.

Your consultants' contracts for services may give them an interest in the settlement money. When this is the case, the consultants' names may also appear on any settlement checks you receive from the insurance company. This will require more endorsements before using the money to pay for repairs.

Contingency Fees

Contingency fees are paid out of the insurance recovery and are *only* paid when you recover. Even though you don't have to pay the professional upfront, the funds you collect will be shared in part with the consultant you hire to protect your interest. This means that the amount of money available to repair your property is reduced.

REAL LIFE EXAMPLE

A new addition on Ralph's home suffered enormous damage when a heavy duty hurricane hit his area. He knew the whole thing would have to be ripped down and replaced, but was slightly concerned that the carrier might deny coverage claiming the addition was not up to code.

Ralph thought it would be best to hire a professional and turn over all of the building plans, receipts and documents to a trained professional. He knew the cost to replace the addition would be $50,000. When the consultant wanted a 20% fee to take on the claim, Ralph realized he'd have to come up with another $10,000 out of pocket to rebuild. He was confident his contractor and architect would hold up under scrutiny if the structure was challenged and he knew he had good documentation. He also knew if he handled the claim himself and won, he'd have more funds to rebuild. In the end, Ralph felt it best to hire a professional only if the claim got denied.

If you pay the professional, will you have enough left to make the repairs you need?

A professional also adds another layer of communication to the claims process. If you hire a lawyer, for example, the insurance company will send all of its communications through him and you will receive it secondhand. If the carrier is pestering you with repeated requests for information, this extra layer can be welcome. But it is also less direct and can slow down the process.

Types of Professionals to Hire

Insurance claims raise questions of causation, damage and valuation, and a homeowner can hire experts to address any of these, from engineers to antiques appraisers. Claimants who decide to bring in an insurance expert frequently choose an attorney or a public adjuster. One other common choice is a general contractor, but for a number of reasons, contractors are not qualified or permitted to do some of the tasks necessary to settling an insurance claim.

Hire a Lawyer

Lawyers are one of the few groups permitted to negotiate a claim on behalf of a policyholder. A skilled lawyer with insurance experience should be able to understand a policy and be up-to-date on legal developments that affect the policy's provisions. Choose an attorney with insurance experience—one versed in your state's insurance regulations and who has experience negotiating claims. Attorneys are licensed by the state in which they practice law but that does not mean they all know that state's insurance rules or understand insurance claims processes.

Lawyers' fee arrangements come in many varieties, including flat fees, hourly rates, and contingency agreements. When they work on a contingency, the policyholder will not need to pay the bills upfront. Instead, the fee comes out of the recovery so there will be less money available to repair or replace the damaged property.

Some insurance carriers indicate in their files when an attorney is involved in a claim. This can trigger a couple of things:

- When an insured is represented by counsel, an insurance company needs to direct information through the lawyer rather than the policyholder. One advantage to the insured is that the carrier is more likely to be on its best behavior when dealing with a lawyer.

- Carriers may become suspicious when a claimant hires an attorney. This can be seen as a red flag that there may be an issue with the claim. If this happens, your case may be put under a microscope and made tougher.

Hire a Public Adjuster

An insurance adjuster is trained to evaluate a claim and determine how much money the insurance company must pay. The claims adjuster works for the insurance company but a **"public adjuster"** is an independent adjuster you can hire to work for you. A public adjuster can review the damage and documentation, prepare an estimate, review your policy and negotiate a payment amount with the insurance company.

Public Adjuster Fees

If a public adjuster is effective, then the award may be larger because of his or her involvement. When it comes to fees:

- They may be structured in a variety of ways with the most common being a contingency agreement.

- Some states require that public adjusters disclose their fees, which can be substantial, upfront.

- If a public adjuster does not explain his fee at the start, make sure you ask.

Regulation of Public Adjusters

Most states regulate public adjusters. Regulations can include:

- **Fee:** Public adjuster commissions are capped at a state-determined percentage of the recovery.

- **Involvement:** Public adjusters must remain independent. They are not permitted to perform or profit from the homeowner's repairs.

- **Registration:** Most states require that public adjusters be licensed and bonded.

It makes sense to hire a public adjuster if the loss is large or the insurance company adjuster is not responsive or has overlooked some damage. Often a public adjuster can get a claim back on track.

The Role of Contractors

Contractors have a complicated place in the claim process. A qualified and experienced general contractor is an excellent person for a homeowner to have involved in the claim. But occasionally contractors improperly step into the role of public adjuster or lawyer, sometimes intentionally and sometimes unintentionally, so a homeowner needs to be on the lookout.

When it comes time to repair damaged property, contractors have valuable input. A respected contractor can be an advocate for necessary repairs and supplements. Insurance-related business tends to be a small universe and if a contractor has insurance remediation experience then he or she likely has some reputation with the insurance companies. If that reputation is positive and trustworthy then the homeowner will benefit.

A Contractor's Second Look Affects the Scope

An insurance carrier's scope is based on the adjuster's non-invasive observation of the property. Once the contractor begins opening up the walls and tearing back the layers of the roof, it is not unusual to find a lot more damage.

A skilled and respected contractor will have the ability to explain the extent of the damages to the adjuster and propose appropriate repairs. He or she can also explain the need for supplemental amounts to cover a rise in materials prices or the increased labor cost that tends to follow a natural disaster, helping to get the payments approved and repairs made more quickly.

Every natural disaster and major storm draws out contractors who tour ravaged neighborhoods representing that they can do the work of a public adjuster. This is illegal. Beware.

If you grant the carrier permission to discuss your claim with a contractor, the contractor can discuss factual issues like the extent of the damage found, what it will cost to repair the damage and other related issues that fall within the realm of his construction expertise. But the contractor cannot argue that damages are covered or represent you in any other policy matter.

Roles of a Public Adjuster vs. Contractors

Keep in mind that contractors are not public adjusters and in most states, cannot negotiate a claim. A contractor may not negotiate as a public adjuster and a public adjuster may not perform or profit from the repairs.

Concluding Thoughts

Often it's only when disaster strikes that people take a good hard look at their homeowner's policy to see what's covered and how to file a claim. Many people don't realize how much the fine print may impact their future.

If you find yourself in a tangle on a homeowner's claim, you may have to get up to speed quickly. This can be fraught with emotional fallout, especially if you've been hit by a natural disaster. If you need help charting a course, or you've done all you can with your insurance carrier or your state insurance department, hire a professional to help you.

Don't be afraid to call in an expert if you do not make progress or feel you are being stonewalled or given the run around by an insurance company. Hiring a public adjuster or an attorney who specializes in these matters may be the best way to get your life back to normal quickly.

Additional Resources

Even when homeowners filing a claim decide to go it alone, there are resources to help with each step.

Better Business Bureau has an online search for businesses. It is great place to check out the reputation of contractors before signing any construction contracts. http://www.bbb.org/

National Association of Public Insurance Adjusters has a registry of member public adjusters who are licensed in their state and have been in business for at least two years. http://www.napia.com/

National Association of Insurance Commissioners links to the insurance department in each state. http://www.naic.org/state_web_map.htm

National Flood Insurance Program provides flood insurance for most areas. To obtain flood insurance, call your insurance agent or contact NFIP at http://www.floodsmart.gov or 1-888-379-9531

Glossary

Actual Cash Value (ACV): For insurance purposes this is the fair market value or the replacement cost (less depreciation) to replace the damaged item with a similar quality item or repair the property with a comparable material.

Arbitration: An alternative dispute resolution method that involves streamlined procedures for submitting evidence and in which a neutral third party called an arbitrator makes a decision according to law and based on the evidence submitted.

Contingency Fees: Legal fees paid to lawyers out of the insurance recovery that are *only* paid when you recover.

Coverages: Section of an insurance policy which lists which losses (if caused by an "occurrence") are covered.

Deductibles: Amount of loss you must incur out of pocket before an insurance claim is paid.

Depreciation: Value lost over time through normal aging, wear and tear, maintenance or neglect, and obsolescence. It can be calculated differently for tax and insurance purposes.

Efficient Proximate Cause: Basis to exclude coverage for a loss because the nearest or most directly responsible cause of the damage is excluded.

Endorsement: A separate legal document added to an insurance contract that provides additional or different terms. It is sometimes called a "rider."

Examination Under Oath (EUO): Sworn statements that have the same weight as testimony in court.

Exclusions: Section of the insurance policy that lists the types of loss that are specifically not covered under the policy.

Glossary

Force-placed/Lender Policies: Insurance purchased to protect a lender's insurable interest in property you own.

Independent Adjuster: Impartial professional who works for an outside company (not your carrier) and reports on amount and extent of damage.

Insurance Bad Faith: Insurance companies owe their policyholders a duty of good faith and fair dealing. When an insurance company breaches this duty, it has engaged in insurance bad faith and you may have a claim in court.

Mediation: Non-binding alternative dispute-resolution method in which a neutral third party, called a mediator, assists two or more parties to negotiate a settlement of their dispute.

Medical Payments Coverage: Insurance clause concerning payment of medical expenses of someone injured on your property.

Occurrence: An accident or unexpected event.

Personal Liability Coverage: Insurance clause concerning payment of claims when someone is injured on your property and you are legally at fault.

Proof of Loss: A sworn statement attesting to the damages with specifics on what caused the loss, who owns the property and dollar amounts for each item of the damage claimed.

Public Adjuster: An independent adjuster (not employed by the insurer) who reviews the damage, documentation and insurance policy, and then prepares an estimate and negotiates a payment amount with the insurance company.

Replacement Cost: The compensation to replace or repair damaged property.

Rider: A document which is used to make changes or add details to the basic legal document. It may be called an "endorsement" if part of an insurance policy.

Scope: This is the estimate of the cost of repairs, also known as the scope of repairs.

Staff Adjuster: Professional who works directly for the insurance carrier to report on damage causing your claim.

Statute of Limitations: Law which provides that a lawsuit must be started within a certain period of time, after an incident or the signing of a contract, or else it can no longer be brought.

About the Author

Dawn Snyder

Dawn Snyder, Esq., is an attorney with a background in civil litigation, including appeals and alternative dispute resolution. Her practice areas include insurance coverage and defense, construction defect, design professional errors and omissions, and personal injury. She received her B.A. from Allegheny College and J.D. from Cleveland-Marshall College of Law and is licensed to practice law in Ohio and Arizona. She is of counsel with Russo & Associates in Fairview Park, Ohio.

About Real Life Legal™

Parker Press Inc., the publisher of Real Life Legal™ creates plain language consumer information on legal, tax, business and financial subjects. Taking aim at info overload and legalese, Parker Press Inc. launched Real Life Legal™ in 2014. Real Life Legal™ provides practical advice, written by lawyers, to help people understand how the law works. Our goal is to provide solid, easy-to-understand information so *you* can decide whether it makes sense to hire a lawyer. Real Life Legal™ wants you to be prepared.

Available Titles

Bankruptcy Basics: Chapter 7 and Chapter 13
Marina Ricci, Esq.

Business Owners Startup Guide
Susan G. Parker, Esq. and Lynne Williams, Esq.

Elder Law: Legal Planning for Seniors
Susan G. Parker, Esq. and Maria B. Whealan, Esq.

Employee's Guide to Discrimination and Termination
Joanne Dekker, Esq.

Estate Planning: A Road Map for Beginners
Susan G. Parker, Esq. and Maria B. Whealan, Esq.

Filing a Homeowner's Claim: Natural Disaster or Not
Dawn Snyder, Esq.

A Lawyer's Guide to Home Renovations
John A. Goodman, Esq.

Available Titles (Continued)

Planning for Pets: Trusts, Leash Laws and More
Joanne Dekker, Esq.

Planning for Your Special Needs Child
Amy Newman, Esq.

Special Needs Education: Navigating for Your Child
Lynne Williams, Esq.

U.S. Veterans: Your Rights and Benefits
Maria B. Whealan, Esq.
with Paul M. Goodson, Esq.

What to Do When Someone Dies
Susan G. Parker, Esq.

You've Been Arrested: Now What?
Maryam Jahedi, Esq.

Notes

Notes

Notes

Notes

Notes

Notes

Notes

Notes

Notes

Notes

Notes

Notes

Notes

Notes

Notes